Service Dog Skills Faster

Timothy Martyn
and
Barbara Miller

Copyright © 2024 Timothy Martyn and Barbara Miller
All rights reserved
First Edition

Fulton Books
Meadville, PA

Published by Fulton Books 2024

ISBN 979-8-88982-833-4 (paperback)
ISBN 979-8-88982-834-1 (digital)

Printed in the United States of America

Foreword

This little book was three years in the making, not because it is a hundred pages long but because of what it took to write it. The lady who came up with the steps, my aunt, did many of them naturally. After over forty years of personally training hundreds of dogs to do some pretty amazing things. In what seems like a five- to ten-minute trick, there are sometimes up to two hundred separate actions. It is not the steps that are hard to understand going forward and backward in sets of three, but that the principles go as a system and have to be done at a specific time, whether you are snapping the dog out of a trance with a teat to the nose or marking a behavior with good at the right time. Many of these things she just did and has told me she looks forward to seeing them in her little book, and I have been like her shadow for three years, watching her do them, asking her questions, and taking notes.

In the last principle I am learning a week before I finish writing, I realize you are not just going through the steps like on the cupboard, but when you show a dog to open a handle from the inside, you just show the dog. Using your eyes to show that it's something to do with the handle, having it put its paw on your hand, and open the door for it, the dog thinks, *Oh, that is what you wanted.*, and are able to do the task itself. Throughout the entire three years, I do not know that the most important part is showing the dog and communicating with it, not just going through the steps with principles. This is the most important principle. With this step, unlike the rest, most other tools are not used; you only show them. But at this point, it has already learned how to open a door, and it is opening a door as well as doing the paw press to have it put its paw on your hand.

I have to thank my aunt for letting me follow her around and giving me the opportunity to learn something that will help people. There are some stories to illustrate the training and methods interchangeably, and most of the stories have videos on the Internet to go with them for you to enjoy.

These steps are done in a set order to get the dog used to working for you before you do things that are harder for the dog to grasp, as well as many of the earlier behaviors used in later behaviors. Go forward one step at a time in sets of three and back when the dog freezes, like in the concept of spiral learning in a psychology class. Go back to the point needed for the dog to go forward again. You need to be shown what it looks like when a dog freezes. Keep in mind all the principles needed for the techniques to work. It all goes bad if you correct, talk, or have bad timing, especially for things like bad timing, not being able to claim space correctly, or not being able to clear your head. You will not be able to use this technique if you are unable to grasp one of these concepts. Especially not being fast enough; if that is the case, you just can't train this way. But if you can and put in the time, it will not only be helpful for you in teaching a skill in ten minutes to an hour, speeding up your overall training time, but it will also be appreciated by many others when you are producing many more dogs with extra skills. Enjoy!

A Sidenote on What We Call Base Steps

What is the first thing a dog needs to determine about any skill or task it can do? Use the correct tool for that task: the nose, teeth, or paw. Once the dog knows the base step, it needs to build on your showing it as a way of explaining the steps and how it can use that base step to do any task you can think of showing it. Like the base step, use your nose. It is always the first step in anything you do using your nose. Turn a light on, shut a door with the nose—anything you can think of that uses the nose, the nose is the base step.

    Next is using the paw. We show the dog when we want it to use its paw in the paw press step. Lowering the hand slowly turns into a command to use its paw. Do it in front of a door or cupboard. It closes the door, and it knows how to close it. From the other side of the door, with a lever handle, show it to use its paw and pow so it can open the door from the inside. The retrieve is the best example of using your teeth once you have shown them they need to use their teeth at the base step. The last step is to put the treat in your hand or on the door when it realize it can open the door. I hope you have fun with this knowledge.

Semantic Encoding Principles, Scaffolding Tools, and Spiral Learning

Here is a definition of semantic encoding:

> Semantic encoding is the cognitive encoding of new information that focuses on its meaningful aspects as opposed to its perceptual characteristics. This will usually involve some form of elaboration. See also deep processing. (APA Dictionary of Psychology)

The following are semantic encoding principles used in all techniques, or one could say scaffolding tools, like in childhood development:

1. *Use the number three.*
    The number of times it needs to be done with understanding to add a small concept to the bigger concept that is forming is three, a learning number even for people. When the dog has done one step correctly three times, move on to the next—the "Rule of Three."
    The way my aunt came across this is an interesting irony. Normally, people do experiments on animals and apply them to people. But in this case, there is some research on people that my aunt saw on a TV special, and she applies it to dogs. We may

think more similarly than we think. Three is also the smallest number to form a link in your mind. This is called chunking.

2. *Don't correct when the dog freezes.*

For you Trekkies: "Watch out, Captain, the episodic buffer is dumping, and the pattern may be lost in transport." (Sometimes information may be lost binding in visual working memory.) In the book, *Exploring Working Memory* (Baddeley, Allen, and Hitch 2017), the study of the role of the episodic buffer shows how the brain has more than one component. Binding memory has many parts and functions, more than we really knew before. More studies on this may lead to many discoveries, not only for our furry friends but for us as well. It is important to note that living creatures are more complicated than we give them credit for. And with dogs in this aspect, it is important to learn to see when a dog is processing and not being difficult or shutting down from stress. Sometimes it's just thinking. As you learn to communicate with your dog, this is a big thing to learn to see and act accordingly.

Our theory goes that, just like people, when information goes from short-term to long-term memory, it gets lost for a second. Try putting a treat in its nose to pull it out. If the problem persists, let it run around for a second, and if necessary, go back a couple of steps. It is important not to interrupt in any way except by scent. Why? I have no clue. Hopefully, someone else can figure it out. But you have to not interrupt the scavenging behavior. Let it run around and look for a treat. And always make sure to have water nearby. Define consummatory, foraging, and scavenging behaviors.

Sidenote: Many of the activities above release serotonin. The levels of serotonin are directly related to aggression. We have seen lower levels of aggression in many dogs, including many Australian shepherds, showing a noticeable difference with their cousins from the same bloodlines.

The study "The Assessment of Serotonin in Dogs" (Kocis et al. 2015) directly shows the balance of serotonin in mood and overall happiness. The main point I am making with this study and the next is that through fun activities, serotonin can increase, which this study implicates can make your dog more well-balanced.

Our skills are ideas and foraging behavior in dogs. According to the study "Activation of Serotonin Neurons Promotes Active Persistence in a Probabilistic Foraging Task" (Lottem et al. 2018), foraging tasks can make animals happier, release serotonin, and help with impulse control.

Luckily, you will be assisting your dog in a foraging task, with each step being a little idea. This leads to the realization of a service dog's skill. Your dog often wants to do it over and over again for fun and demands a treat. This is to be encouraged.

3. *Once they do it correctly for that step, never accept a lesser offer.*
Never let anyone—your kid, your dog, especially yourself—get a reward for being lazy. This bad habit not only ruins your training session, it can also ruin your life. Once it does it right, keep going forward if you can. Go back only if it freezes.

4. *There is no correction at all during the learning process.*
Throw out all these: No corrections, just no rewards. Don't give a treat if the dog does it wrong. Stay positive. Negativity shuts down the learning process. Instead of freezing, where the dog is still trying but has forgotten how for a second or more, it just shuts down because its brain is tired, which looks different. Corrections can cause a different kind of shutdown when it tries to learn if you correct it before it knows what you want. These sessions can last an hour, not just fifteen minutes, when you can see that its brain has not run out of power.

Corrections are for a dog that knows what it is doing and why it is getting corrected. You want to be at the forefront of its mind, not on whether you will correct it but on the idea being presented. This process uses its entire brainpower. It cannot be worrying about two things. When it knows the idea and what it is being corrected for, you often only have to correct it once.

5. *Don't talk the dog through it.*
   Let the dog try to figure it out. Reward the action with an immediate treat when it does it right. Don't distract the dog with a bunch of words. Speak only to give the command and mark the behavior you want. Remember to communicate with your eyes, like in step seven, orienting them to the cupboard with your body language. Not calming the space like in step ten and touching its nose with a teat to redirect and when it needs a better treat when frozen may snap the dog out of it. Claim the space for animals and dogs.

6. *Use the word good with a purpose.*
   Use the word like a clicker to mark a behavior, but not just the behavior—the understanding of the idea. If you can't get the treat there fast enough to mark the behavior fast enough for the dog to figure out the idea being presented in that step, the dog will not learn. Also, if it is confused, start showing the right behavior to guide it in that direction. In these times, the dog will be looking to you for guidance and concept learning.

7. *Eye contact*
   A dog pays attention to your eyes and reads your intentions. Make sure your eyes are telling the dog what you want. As if having a conversation, look at the dog, and then, with your intention, look at the object of learning. And do not divide your thoughts on what you want them to do. Research where a person is looking.
   Things to know when using your eyes:
   a. Try not to make eye contact. The dog will stop and wonder what you want from it until you give an indicator and stay if you sustain eye contact.
   b. What I mean by indicator is looking and showing intention toward the object or task you want the dog to do or figure out. You will be surprised at how well your dog can read you if you communicate your intentions correctly.

Here is a study on your eyes: "Eye Contact Is Crucial for Referential Communication in Pet Dogs" (Savalli, Resende, and Gaunet 2016). This study shows the many important ways dogs use their eyes.

Often, you can look at your dog and look at the object of training, or you can look at them and look at the ground to either let it know that there is a tug to pull or to lay down. Things like holding eye contact too long can lead to a staring contest. Sometimes what seems obvious to us means something different to the dog.

8. *Clearing your mind so the dog does not get mixed signals.*

    If you are thinking about your bad day and feeling nervous, the dog will pick up on that. Remember that dogs can smell your fear. However, you need to be calm and confident, and most importantly, clear your mind of all outside distractions and only have the intention of the action in your head. The dog will pick up on your nonverbal body language of wanting it to do the task at hand, not your stress. Can you convey what you want and your intentions this way to an animal?

    A study on smelling your fear, "Epilepsy and the Smell of Fear" (Maa, Arnold, and Bush 2021), shows that dogs really pick up your different states of being. If you are afraid, they smell it. If you're stressed, they'll know. If you're distracted, what's that? Dogs really need you to be focused. Dogs can indeed smell your fear.

9. *Try to only do one concept (task) for the most sticking power in the puppy's head.*

10. *Claim your space wisely. (You should claim space in some situations and not others.)*

    To explain further, practice calming your space in the kitchen and doorway, not claiming your space, and letting them through. If you claim the object you are trying to teach a behavior, the dog will not work for you. You have to be *aware* of this.

There is a study on this titled "Studies in Personal Space" (Sommer 1959, 247–260). As you know, personal space is important in your life. It is also important for your dog. Whether it is guarding a bone there, working together like their ancestors did, deciding where to lie down, or how to hunt, you need to become aware of what you are communicating to your dog and use it to help you. Teach it.

11. *Always put the object of thought in its field of vision when it thinks about it.*

    Be aware of its field of vision; don't block it. How do you know when it thinks about it? Whether it is lying down while doing the cupboard or sitting and looking at your hand for the light switch, it has to know what it is working on.

    Many scientists believe animals think small thoughts that lead to concepts. We act on this principle, with each step being a concept led by many little ideas. Here is a study on this debate: "How Dogs Know When Communication Is Intended for Them" (Kaminski, Schulz, and Tomasello 2011). This is another study that shows the many ways dogs can communicate. Words, eye contact, and body language—you must be aware of all these things.

12. *Engage its nose with a treat and have it look at your eyes, and with your eyes, orient it to the object of learning when the dog's attention wanders and it loses concentration.*

    This is the *only* thing you can do to gain attention if the dog gets distracted, looks for an easier treat, etc. Do not wiggle anything or talk unnecessarily, which will further distract the dog.

13. *Most importantly, you can't just go through the steps. You have to have the attention of the dog and communicate with it. You are showing the dog something, not just going through steps.*

    Interactive communication: here is a study on using the eyes to communicate in dogs entitled "How Dogs Know When

Communication Is Intended for Them" (Kaminski, Schulz, and Tomasello 2011). This study shows how well dogs can read us. You can learn to read them over time. I believe it creates a new language for you and your dog.

Many of these principles may have to be taught separately, but if you can see it, they are all used sometimes at the same time, sometimes separately, but as a unit. And they all go together. And if you are having trouble with one, you may want to work on it by itself.

Paw Press

When doing the paw press, it is very important not to hover over the dog and claim its space. Make sure to remember this, or it won't be learned. Where do we stand, and what is our posture? Use of hands.

After you have taught the paw press like a puzzle (something to figure out), you will notice an interesting side effect. There is a private lesson where a lady has a border collie that freaks out in the car and just goes nuts whenever it moves. For some reason, when you teach the paw press this way and teach it to a dog in that state of mind, you will notice an extreme calming effect. In about fifteen minutes on three visits, the dog calms completely. With only doing the paw press to get it to calm down. It's always nice to have good side effects. Is there scientific evidence for this? It goes from the right side of the brain to the left. Is there research, or can you propose research?

Paw Press Story

There are many good uses for how we teach the paw press. It is the first thing we teach. I trained my dog, Xiler, to open the cupboard many years ago. Because it already knows the paw press, we are able to transfer it to close the cupboard and the door with its paw. Either the dog or you close the door. It realizes that it has just shut the door of the cupboard. It can be transferred to a real door quickly.

Slowly lowering the fist turns into a command, which can be turned into opening the door when there is a lever.

It is fun videoing my dog, getting the remote across the room out of the cupboard, and having my dog really know what I want. With a little lowering of my fist in the air and running across the room to shut the door, it truly understands.

The first step is the paw press. Directions for later use: pushing, closing the cupboard door, or anything else; switching a hyper puppy to thinking instead of just reacting; and tricks like wave, shake hands, etc. These apply to other types of training tools.

Steps:

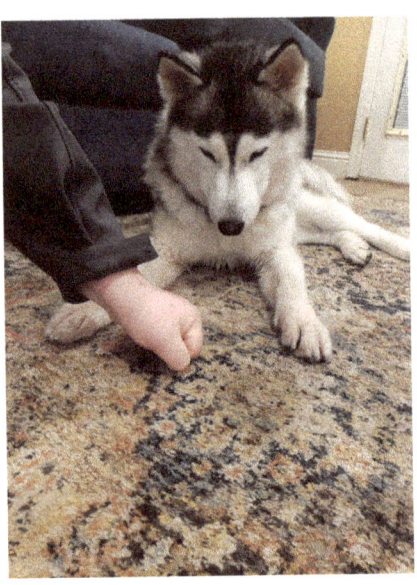

SERVICE DOG SKILLS FASTER

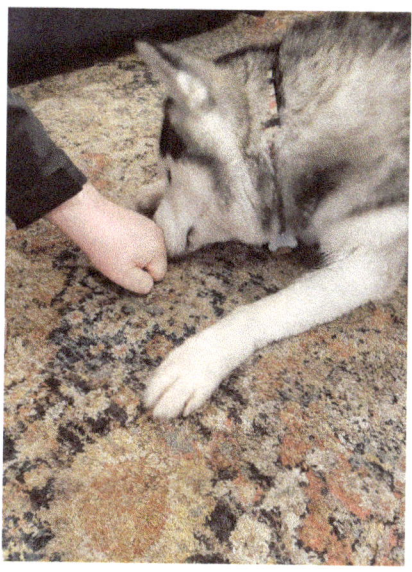

1. Get a treat and put it in your hand in front of the dog on the floor.

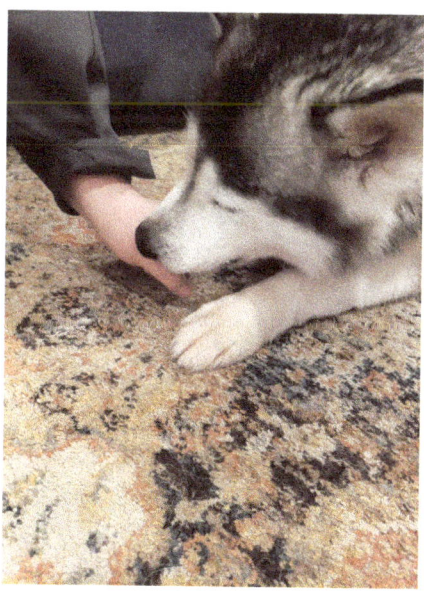

2. Move it around in front of the dog if it likes to chase. (Often called prey drive, but behaviorists don't like that term.) If the dog is smelling and licking, hold the treat still. This puts the dog in a scavenging state of mind. You need to keep it in this state of mind to get the effect.

3. When the dog touches it with its paw, quickly give it a treat.

Note: If it takes a good amount of time for the dog to figure out that you want it to touch you with its paw, touch the paw with your hand and give it a treat. Is the dog copying you? Cite new and old research—"Do as I Do?"

4. Slowly lower the hand with the treat to the floor. When the anticipation (in animals) is high and the dog hits your hand before it reaches the floor, give it a treat.

SERVICE DOG SKILLS FASTER

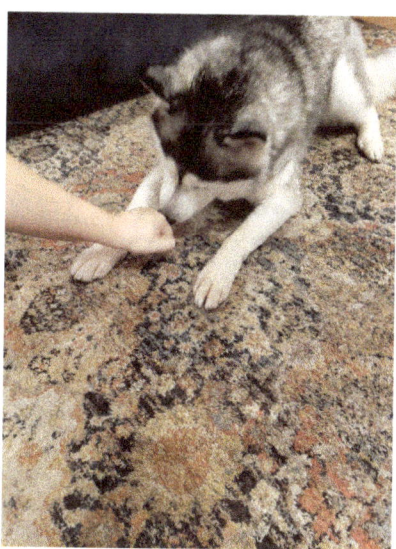

5. Slowly raise the height. *The most important thing* is that if they freeze, only snap the dog out with a treat and keep water nearby. You will notice that it wants an easy treat and will be sniffing around for one. It is still in scavenging mode, but its information is lost. Back up a bit. Let it drink water and sniff, and when it comes back, often the information is learned and present. If you do not let it process, you might as well not be doing it this way. You will lose all the positive learning side effects. The idea is lost, and it will not transfer to shutting a door or help its mind prepare for harder concepts.

6. An opportunity to target a trick: (a) Wave when the dog does a couple of high-up swings, and give it a treat; (b) when the dog does it, attach the word by saying it.

Another Trick: Low Five

Lower the hand without the treat. Flip it over, and when the dog hits it, give a treat with the other hand. Attach the word by saying it when the dog does it.

That's it for paw press until we teach you to use it to shut the door in the service dog section. Keep in mind that this can be used and practiced to calm down a hyper dog.

Story for Down

Down is one of the funniest techniques to teach in my aunt's system. It is the first thing I learn. Some of the steps are the ones you see in other methods like luring and a hand signal, but using your eyes, the nod of a dog's head, or getting it to offer a behavior are new to me.

My aunt brings in a border collie, goes through the steps, and then hands the dog to me. I say down, and bam, the dog goes down. Barbara says, "Good, keep training." I say, "No, I do not catch on to half your steps, but the dog knows it now. Teach me."

When you do the steps correctly the first time, the dog should know the command from the first session.

The following are the steps for down:

1. Touch the dog's nose with a treat.

2. Lure the dog to the floor three successful times.

3. When the dog gives an indication that it is going to go down, drop it to the floor. This can look like eyes looking down or a

bend in the elbow. Make sure you are looking at the floor to show the dog what you want.

Look down when the dog offers the behavior; attach the word and give the treat. Attach the word by saying it at the same time you do it.

This skill may be harder to do for some people. It requires reading the dog thoroughly. Do not be discouraged. It is not necessary for more advanced service dog skills.

Story for Sit

Sit is the most basic command, but it can have good uses. I am lucky enough to grow up with many litters of puppies. From the very start, you can teach puppies and your older dogs to sit and be petted.

One client has a two-year-old kid with her, and the yard dogs break loose and run a streak for the little guy. The mom screams and runs toward the kid. The dogs get there first, and they all run up and sit. a useful tool just for teaching a dog to sit to be petted.

The Sit

1. Position yourself exactly in front of the dog.

2. Get its attention for half a second by wiggling the treat.

3. Lure the dog with a hand signal, about half a foot out, straight up to your sternum.

Swing

Story for Swing

This command can be turned into one of the funniest commands. My aunt Barbara's son, my cousin Jim, has a dog named Gus, which passed away a little while ago. That dog has won nationals for Australian Shepherd Club of America with Jim. But what I remember most is how he taught his dog to swing. It is so happy to swing that it jumps in the air and lands in heel position on its side. It is very happy to do whatever you ask it to do, but it really loves the swing. This can be more fun than jumping for problem dogs if introduced correctly.

This is broken into two separate segments done in separate sessions.

1. Get the attention of the dog.

2. Left arm and left leg step back and lure back at the same time out in a circle, then toward your leg, a foot out brings them up to sit.

3. Repeat until the dog does this consistently. This will be its hand signal.

4. Say the word first, then do the motion to attach it.

Possible Behaviors to Target

The dog may jump into position if you like this behavior. Give it a treat, so it continues. This concludes the first four behaviors: stay and come can be done now, as can the first step of service dog work in the cupboard.

Stay

Stay Story

Such a little thing, but the idea, "I am coming back with a treat. Stay there," can speed your dog's training time. Some people do short-stay commands at a small distance. Some people put the dog back with the lease they break. There are many ways. But just the idea, "I'm coming back with a treat," can be so helpful.

Stay means I am coming right back with a treat. With the dog seated beside you, say "Stay." Step in front, repeat "Stay," and step back beside it and give it a treat. Never call it off; "Stay" always comes right back with a treat. The rest can be done with the method of your choice (service dog methods).

The Cupboard

The example of the cupboard I am using is with a young journalism student named Andrew Turck at the time at the University of Montana. He needs a story for a class; I still get to hear about the fun stuff he is reporting on when he calls. I agree to show him how to get a dog to open the cupboard, which takes ten minutes to an hour. I bring the cupboard to the house where his roommate has a corgi. I do not have time to teach the paw press ahead of time, which makes it a lot easier. Plus the fact that the corgi has fear issues, so I cannot do the steps myself. I have to talk him through it from the other room. There is one mistake—he is giving the treat to the dog instead of letting the dog scavenge for it to get it out of the cloth. After explaining the concept, he is the one who catches it, and after exactly an hour, about the longest time a skill can take, the dog is opening the cupboard over and over again for fun and demanding treats. At this point, the owner of the dog walks through and jokes about the dog opening the door. I tell him that now the dog is used to me, and that takes about twenty minutes. This is when he decides he doesn't want the dog to always get in his stuff. I am looking forward to seeing his article in a dog magazine.

As a guideline, it is important to make sure the dog digs the treat out itself. Do not get it out for them. It is like it is scavenging for food. As always, remember all the principles going forward and backward in sets of three, etc.

1. Put the treat in the cupboard and let the dog get it. This shows there is a treat inside that they are scavenging for.

2. Put the treat in the opening of the cupboard and shut the door with the treat partly sticking out. When the dog tries to pull it out in the beginning, you open the cupboard. This shows the dog that it can use its teeth to get the treat.

3. After three times, let the dog get the treat. Let it take a little more effort to get the treat. This suggests that there might be a slight obstacle afterward.

4. Wrap it in a tug where you can partially wrap the treat in the tug, like a hot dog, where the animal can get the treat but has to touch the wrap. This lets it know that overcoming the obstacle has something to do with the wrap.

5. Have the treat wrapped in the tug, but held on the other side of the door. Open when it just pulls on it. The dog has to get it out itself; it has to know its job. This shows that pulling on the wrap can get the dog its food and that it is still scavenging for its treat.

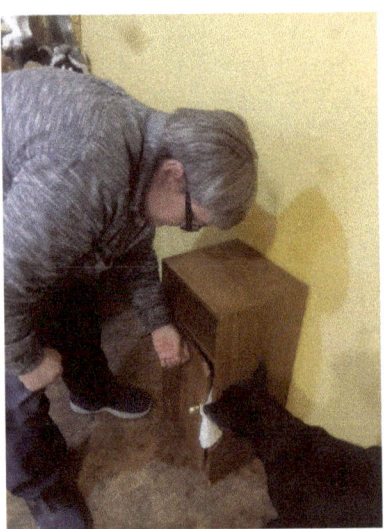

6. Do the same as step 5 but only when the dog pulls it open for itself. It doesn't get it yet, but at some level it will notice the door opening.

7. Put the treat inside with a knot and let the dog open it. When it tugs and there is a knot and it goes, "Wow, the door opens," and it can get the treat inside, this is when it connects all the other concepts and realizes, "I can open a cupboard." When it is excited and does the task again and again, do step 8.

8. (They have to see the treat land for this step.) Tie the tug to the handle, throw the treat inside, and shut the door. The dog will expect yummies. You may do this step untell you or the dog are bored.

Shutting the door with a paw press can now be introduced. Now that the dog knows that it can open a door, shutting it is a piece of cake. Shut the door with a paw press.

After I have done the previous steps with my dog, Xyler, this is a piece of cake. It knows that the hand signal means shut the door; you just have to show it how. There are no steps for this; just one idea. As well as lowering your fist, which is the signal to do it above the handle. It hits the handle and your hand, opening the door. YOU GOT IT! This is what a base step can do. Anything a paw can do can be shown this way.

1. Do the paw press by the open door of the cupboard. The door is open by two inches.

2. When the dog hits your hand or the door and you shut the door, give a treat at the click of the cupboard.

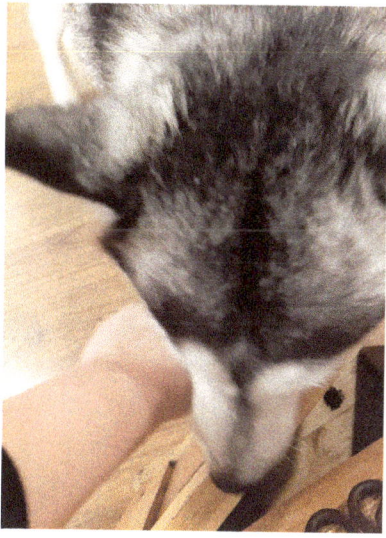

3. Do the paw press signal, but move your hand away from the door and give the treat at the click of the cupboard.

When the dog understands, it opens and closes the door itself a few times. Let it do this while it is processing something. Throw a treat in if you wish to encourage the new behavior.

For example, for this skill, my uncle tells me a story about a hound named Rattler. My aunt and uncle are walking around the property, discussing which dogs have trouble learning. They think that because the hound is obsessive about scent, it may give her some trouble. After about half an hour, the dog not only learns the cupboard but also transfers to the door in the same session before running out of brain power. Remember, the dog tells you when your session is over, and normally, it only does one concept per session, but the door and the cupboard are the same concept: opening the door, and if their brain can last, go for it.

After showing your dog how to open a cupboard, next is opening other things—the most useful is the door. The dog knows how to do it on the cupboard, so you get that tug and put it on the rope at the door. Even my aunt's little chihuahua, Chicka, understands the proper steps. And it takes even less time than opening the cupboard. Have the little dog come over; let it see a treat thrown in the door, and it will open it happily.

Transferring It to the Door

1. Go to the door and take the tug from the cupboard; put a knot in it.

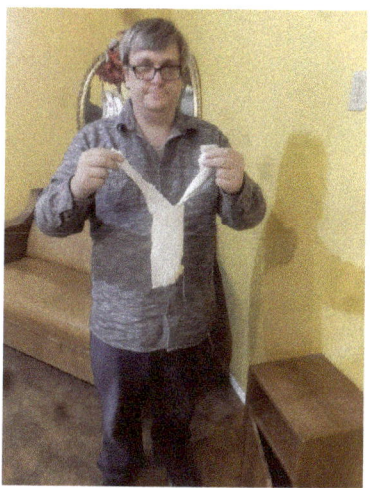

2. Hold the dog. Let it see that you put the treat on the other side of the door. Put the rag at the height of the cupboard knob first. When it touches the rag with its teeth, open the door.

3. Only give the treat when they pull.

4. Put a long cloth on the handle. If they kind of bite, open the door.

5. This is when the dog opens the door itself. Put the treat where they can see it, and shut the door. If it has trouble, go back a step or two. The dog knows that it is opening something because you have shown them that concept on the cupboard, and you showed them that way. When the dog does it on its own by pulling when it is tied to the handle, it knows.

The Retrieve

So to start off an example of learning the retrieve, we use the example of one of my aunt's friends. She has trained with my aunt for many years, and she is never able to teach the retrieve that way. Later, after I am more familiar with the idea of claiming space, I am able to show her. The next day, she sends Barbara pics of her being able to use her retrieve method. She is so happy.

This is the main mistake with many of these techniques. Don't claim where the dog is trying to learn. You can tell by watching the animal in question. The dog respects your bubble. You often have to draw on yourself. I practice this with a dog and a cookie—not a dog cookie, a real cookie. Put it in front of you and claim your space.

The dog tests you at first, but it will soon respect that the cookie is yours. Then stop claiming it and let it have the cookie. This shows you often how to claim and not claim an object.

There is a video of this that shows my aunt at her friend Betty's house having her son's service dog retrieve objects he points the laser at from across the room. This is very useful when there are many objects to remember.

Steps:

1. Take a regular old obedience dumbbell. The dog does not associate with toys. This shows you are showing it something like before, not playing.

2. Touching the side of the dog's nose gives it a treat to introduce the object.

3. Give the dog a treat when it touches the object, which leads to them showing initiative toward that object.

4. Have the dog touch the middle, which starts to show it should pick the object up.

5. Here is the tricky part: don't give the dog the treat unless it touches it with its teeth on its own. You CANNOT put it in its mouth. But you can have the treat behind the dumbbell, an inch back, where they touch their teeth on their own. *It has to understand itself. Do not force this part.* When you see that it understands and does it three times, that is when the first idea is realized.

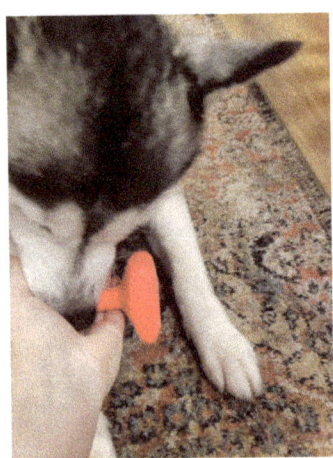

6. Lower the object slowly three times, at least a foot each time.

7. This is the most important part. Make sure the dog doesn't think you are claiming the object. Put it on the ground, and when the dog gets it with its teeth, scoop it with your hand and give the dog a treat. Then the dog knows it goes in your hand, and the movement you used in picking it up is the command that you can attach a word to later. Step 9 shows that your hand can be anywhere; bring it there.

8. Practice putting your hand in other places a little at a time.

9. Add the extra objects you introduce to them in order of hardness if they are similar. The dog knows that you want the object from the base step, so just put some thought into which objects are similar and how hard they are to retrieve and put them in order.

Use a laser to tell them which object you want, so you don't have to use words.

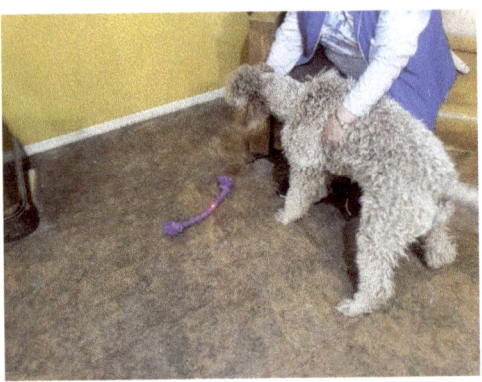

1. Use the retrieve command on an object right next to another object.

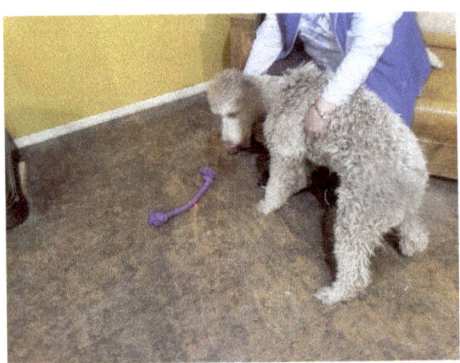

2. Only give the treat when the object with the laser pointer is given.

3. Use your eyes to indicate what you want.

4. They figure it out.

Light Switch

The example for this skill is a dog that, at the moment, is a puppy and has been videotaped along the way. This skill is taught differently, depending on how smart your dog is. If it is smart, you teach it to turn the light switch on, and at this point in learning things, it figures out how to turn it off. This is an example of that. If it is not as smart, you have to teach a tug.

When Rudy Travis's puppy, a miniature Australian shepherd, learns the light, it is very enthusiastic. By the time it is on the wall, jumping on the chair, and turning on the light, it starts messing with it, turning it on and off to get an extra treat. At this point, no command is used to turn off the light. Then in a practice session, my aunt is making it shut the door and the cupboard. Then she told Travis to say, "Light shut shutting," meaning use your paw. It looks at him like, "What?" then runs over, jumps on the chair, and turns off the light.

Light Switch

The newest example of this is the newest video my friend Jae put online. After learning the steps quickly from my aunt, a few segments are put online, clearly showing one of the steps in one video of him lowering a handheld light switch and the dog flipping the switch. The most important part to know in this is the first step—putting your hand in a way that your dog figures out that you need to use your nose. Many of those videos go viral on Instagram. I am hoping I can explain all this in a way that many can understand.

1. The first step is done without a light switch. Put your hand flat in front of the dog's nose. Get the treat in the other hand an inch down and directly underneath the index finger. You know you are doing right if they have to push up on your hand to get the treat.

2. Do the same with one finger.

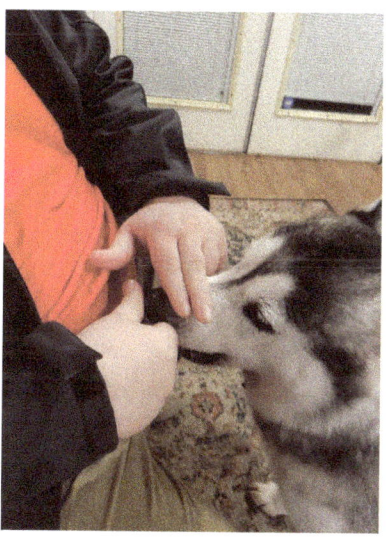

3. Repeat with a pencil.

4. Repeat with a handheld light switch.

Get yourself a light switch, and when the dog turns on the switch, turn on the actual switch so it knows that the light switch turns on the light. Then raise it up, and when it reaches the right height, use the actual light.

Touch for the Door Button, Emergency Button, etc.

An example of this is a video of a service dog long ago named Ginger in a place poorly designed for people in wheelchairs in the Vo-Tech in Montana. There is a place with double doors where, if it is not timed, the dog and the person can get stuck between the doors. It shows the dog quickly pushing one button after the other so they get through smoothly and don't get stuck.

Button Push

You have to use your nose for the base idea here. Poker chips are first used to show the dog this, then the button itself. I see a dog, which my aunt placed and trained over twenty years ago, in an old video pushing one button, letting the other person through, then pressing the next in a double door. The dog truly knows what it is doing. This works for an emergency button, a door, or anything else you can think of. Once it knows how to press the button, you can attach any meaning. And use the nose for any command you can think of that uses the nose.

1. Touch a poker chip to the dog's nose and give it a treat.

2. When the dog touches the poker chip, give it a treat.

3. Get a handheld handicap button and let the dog push it. Give the treat at the click of a button. The sound makes it realize that an action has been accomplished.

4. Transfer to the door. Put it on the door. Let the dog see the treat on the other side. When it pushes the button, open the door.

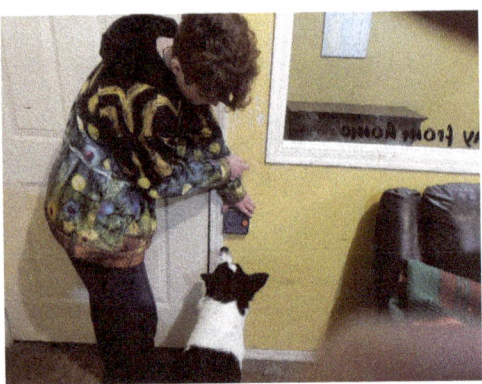

5. Have the dog do it at the actual door button.

An Emergency Button

No matter if it is a tug, a button push, or a paw press, give the reward for the result of the action, whether it is a blinking light, a dial tone, or anything else.

Then attach the word. By saying it with the action, whether it be help or any other word or action, the dog has to know the concept. With the commands before, they can be transferred to the new command.

The dog has to know the paw press and cupboard and know how to think for itself before this can be taught. The dog has to know that it is getting help by pushing the button in that situation. Simulate and have them push and get a treat; the dog will know when to do it. At first, the dog knows it as any other action to take, but with the one who is its person, it will know that it really needs help. And in cases like a diabetic alert dog, where we have taught a dog to bring a juice box to the site of an attack, they will smell the blood sugar dropping and bring the juice box ahead of time.

Teach the chain of behaviors for this complex task. The dog knows how to open and shut cupboards first and retrieve things from them. Introduce objects like a small fridge that is like a cupboard to the dog. It will open the door and shut it right away. Introduce retrieving a juice box and putting it into the fridge. We will be going over alerts in the next book. But when he alerts to, in this case, low blood sugar, have the dog follow this behavior chain. Some of the service dogs my aunt trained for this will figure out that their blood sugar is dropping and get a juice box before the attack.

I hope you enjoy this and have lots of fun with your pups. The next book will cover alerts—hearing, diabetes, PTSD, anxiety, etc.

Take care!

About the Author

Timothy Martyn wrote *Service Dog Skills Faster* with the goal of shortening the time taken to train service dogs. It was written and contributed by Timothy and created by his aunt, Barbara Miller.

When his aunt was young, she trained dogs in her own way. When his aunt was twenty-two, she wanted to compete in obedience. She took an obedience class from Timothy's father, D. Glenn Martyn, who now teaches at Bergin University, runs the hearing dog program and the fire wind training kennels, where Timothy grew up.

Barbara took three dogs and threw Timothy's dad's class at the same time, taking turns fifty years ago. Then she competed in her first obedience competition with all three dogs, one of which, out of novice A, got a 99.5 and tied for high in the trail. And after three competitions, all three won the CD title.

They trained together for a long time—police dogs, tracking dogs, hearing dogs, and service dogs. They trained together in the first service dog program in Montana—Pawsabilities, which started as a department of a community medical center in Missoula, Montana.

Then his aunt started Karosel Service Dogs, where she perfected faster methods with dogs that were not bred for service dog work. All kinds of dogs helped her perfect her methods, which was handy if a person wanted to train or have their own dog trained if suitable.

Next was the herding competition. His aunt came up with new methods for teaching herding. With her first dog, Taylor, the first-time trew got second in nationals. Her husband won nationals in the open, and her son Jim later won nationals in the advanced. They all very much enjoyed playing the herding game together.

He grew up at a kennel, training cats when he was four. His kitties would heal, sit, stay, come, lie down, roll over, and stand up.

One would retrieve, and one would jump from shoulder to shoulder. He would work them around the dogs in training so the dogs would learn not to chase the cats.

He worked with field and police dogs, obedience dogs, and problem dogs. He was too little to do the police dog sleeve, but some of his funniest memories were doubling back on his trail and hiding to teach them to air-send.

That led to this, where he had been helping his aunt put her method into a form where it could be taught to others.

Printed in the USA
CPSIA information can be obtained
at www.ICGtesting.com
CBHW040027250924
14725CB00095B/891